Humanitarian Organisations

Red Cross

Ann Parry

For Jack and Win Parry—exceptional and loving parents.

First published in 2005 by
MACMILLAN EDUCATION AUSTRALIA PTY LTD
627 Chapel Street, South Yarra 3141

Visit our website at www.macmillan.com.au

Associated companies and representatives throughout the world.

National Library of Australia
Cataloguing-in-Publication data

Parry, Ann, 1949–.
Red Cross.

Includes index.
For upper primary school students.
ISBN 0 7329 9740 2.

1. Red Cross – Juvenile literature. I. Title. (Series: Parry, Ann, 1949– Humanitarian organisations).

361.77

Edited by Angelique Campbell-Muir and Anna Fern
Cover and text design by Raul Diche
Maps by Pat Kermode
Photo research by Legend Images

Printed in China

Acknowledgements
The author and the publisher are grateful to the following for permission to reproduce copyright material:

Cover photographs: Red Crescent volunteers assisting victims in Dafur, Sudan, courtesy of the International Committee of the Red Cross. The Weather Coast Assessment Relief Team, courtesy of the Australian Red Cross. The Red Cross supplies food to children in Kosovo, courtesy of the Australian Red Cross.

AAP/AP Photo/Louis Lanzano, p. 25; Amnesty International, p. 4 (logo); Australian Red Cross, pp. 1, 4 (logo), 6, 7, 8, 9, 10, 15, 16, 18, 20, 22, 23, 26, 27, 28, 29, 30; L. Lynch/Australian Red Cross, p. 11; Australian Red Cross/A. McColl/Federation, p. 19; Australian Volunteers International, p. 4 (logo); Doctors Without Borders/Médecins Sans Frontières (MSF), p. 4 (logo); Cindy Ehlers, Animal Assisted Crisis Response Team Training, and PAAWS (www.peopleandanimalswhoserve.org), p. 17; Greenpeace, p. 4 (logo); International Committee of the Red Cross, pp. 5, 14; Picture Media/Reuters/Marc Serota, p. 21; Save the Children, p. 4 (logo); Merritt "Chip" Screiber, p. 24.

While every care has been taken to trace and acknowledge copyright, the publisher tenders their apologies for any accidental infringement where copyright has proved untraceable. Where the attempt has been unsuccessful, the publisher welcomes information that would redress the situation.

Please note
At the time of printing, the Internet addresses appearing in this book were correct. Owing to the dynamic nature of the Internet, however, we cannot guarantee that all these addresses will remain correct.

Contents

Glossary words

When a word is printed in **bold**, its meaning is included on that page. You can also look up its meaning in the Glossary on page 31.

What is a humanitarian organisation?

Humanitarian organisations work to help solve problems in countries around the world, wherever there is a need for their help. They are sometimes called aid agencies, not-for-profit or non-government organisations (NGOs). Some organisations, such as Greenpeace, work to protect the environment. Others, such as Amnesty International and the International Red Cross, work to protect people's **human rights** or provide for their basic needs in times of conflict and disaster. Doctors Without Borders sends **volunteers** anywhere in the world to give medical help to people affected by disasters. Groups like Save the Children and Australian Volunteers International help rebuild communities that need food, education and advice.

Some humanitarian organisations are given money by governments to help run their programs. They also work hard to collect enough money from the public to keep going. Some of their workers are volunteers and are not paid, while others work for a small wage.

The *Humanitarian Organisations* series focusses on six well-known organisations and explains how they help those in need around the world.

Glossary words

humanitarian
devoted to people's welfare and the promotion of social reform

human rights
a set of rights, such as the right to a fair trial, laid down by the United Nations

volunteers
people who donate their time to a cause

australianvolunteers
international

Australian Volunteers International

The Red Cross

Greenpeace

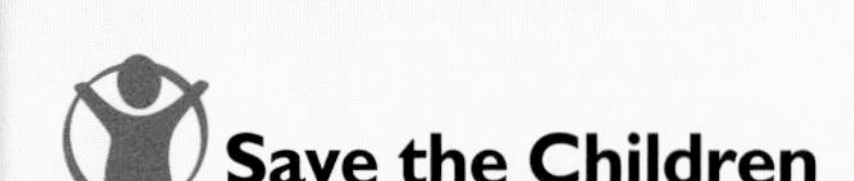

Save the Children

Amnesty International

Doctors Without Borders

About the Red Cross

Some countries, such as those with Muslim cultures, prefer to use the Red Crescent symbol.

The International Red Cross and Red Crescent Movement is the largest international humanitarian organisation in the world. It is made up of three parts: the International Federation of Red Cross and Red Crescent Societies, the International Committee of the Red Cross, and the National Red Cross or Red Crescent Societies (in 181 countries around the world).

This is the logo of the International Committee of the Red Cross.

The International Federation of Red Cross and Red Crescent Societies

The International Federation of Red Cross and Red Crescent Societies coordinates help for the victims of natural disasters, undertakes **community development** and advises national societies. It is independent of government and has no connections with any particular political, religious or cultural group. This is extremely important in allowing them to do their work without interference, when people need help.

The International Committee of the Red Cross

The International Committee of the Red Cross (ICRC) helps victims of armed conflict. It is the guardian of the **Geneva Conventions** and makes decisions about the rules of war.

As well as the International Red Cross, there are 181 national societies, in countries around the world, which choose a Red Cross or Red Crescent as their symbol. These national societies help people in their own country. They may also, if directed by the International Red Cross, work in other countries and cooperate with other aid organisations. The societies deliver food, shelter and basic medical care, support other emergency workers who are involved in rescues, and provide many local programs and services. Most of the money to run programs comes from public donations and from business partnerships.

The American Red Cross gives aid to more than 600 000 disaster victims each year.

Glossary words

community development
the building of stronger communities (e.g. through help for women's groups or support for teenagers)

Geneva Conventions
ways of behaving in wars (e.g. towards prisoners) accepted and agreed to by the countries that have signed the documents

History of the Red Cross

The International Red Cross was formed more than 140 years ago. In 1859, a Swiss businessman called Henri Dunant came upon the results of a terrible battle between French and Austrian soldiers in Solferino, northern Italy. Young men were suffering and dying with no one to help them. Dunant arranged for some of the local people to take care of the wounded from both armies, before he returned to Switzerland. The help given on the battlefield during those days, such as first aid, **neutral** assistance to all parties involved in the conflict, and the taking and delivering of Red Cross messages, continues to this day. It is still some of the core work of the Red Cross.

The International Committee of the Red Cross

Dunant held a meeting in Geneva in 1863 that set up the International Committee for Relief to the Wounded. This was to become the International Committee of the Red Cross. The Red Cross encouraged the Swiss government to hold the conference that developed the first Geneva Convention in 1864. This was the first attempt to form rules for behaviour in wars. In particular, these rules stated that soldiers and civilians were to be treated **humanely**, and that medical staff should be regarded as 'neutral'.

The Red Cross symbol, a red cross on a white background, is the inverse of the Swiss flag. It represents hope and help around the world.

The shocking sight of wounded soldiers at the Battle of Solferino is what prompted Henri Dunant to begin his humanitarian work.

Glossary words

neutral
not taking either side in an argument or fight

humanely
considerately, compassionately

The Red Cross was awarded the Nobel Prize for Peace three times in recognition of its humanitarian work.

The International Federation of Red Cross and Red Crescent Societies

After World War I (1914–18), the League of Red Cross Societies (which was later named the Federation of Red Cross and Red Crescent Societies) was founded, to work on improving the health of those affected by the fighting.

Henry Davidson, the President of the American Red Cross War Committee, suggested at an international medical conference that a federation of Red Cross societies be formed. In 1919, the League of Red Cross Societies was formed.

Today, millions of people are members of what is now called the International Federation of Red Cross and Red Crescent Societies (the name was changed in 1991). It is the largest humanitarian group in the world, with societies in almost every country. The Red Cross helps people in more than 80 relief operations every year and has nearly 100 million volunteer workers. One hundred and eighty-nine countries have now signed the Geneva Conventions, which have been promoted by the Red Cross since its beginning.

Nobel Prize for Peace honours

The International Committee of the Red Cross has been awarded the **Nobel Prize for Peace** in both 1917 and 1944, with a joint award to the Committee and the Federation in 1963. This prize is awarded by the famous Nobel Foundation, in Norway, and is only presented to very special people or groups.

Glossary word

Nobel Prize for Peace
an award presented by the Nobel Committee in Sweden to a person or group who gives the greatest benefit to humankind

Did you know?

Some countries with a high proportion of non-Christian religions, such as Hinduism or Islam, prefer to use the Red Crescent symbol. This is because the cross could be taken as a sign of Christianity.

The founder of the International Red Cross

Henri Dunant grew up in a family that believed in the tradition of religion, care for others and duty to the community. When Henri came across the dreadful sights at the Battle of Solferino, he felt it was his duty to take the lead in arranging all the help he could for the wounded. In 1862, he published a small book about his experiences, called *A Memory of Solferino*. This book was to make him famous.

Henri Dunant was the founder of the Red Cross.

In his book, Henri emphasised the need for an international cooperative group of trained volunteers, who should be recognised and protected in their work, to help in any such future disasters.

Dunant gets help

Henri was not a great organiser, but he was a very persuasive speaker. A man called Gustav Moynier, chairman of the Geneva Society for Public Welfare, read *A Memory of Solferino* and formed a committee to work on Dunant's ideas. It was the committee that arranged the 1864 international conference, which developed the first Geneva Convention and, later, the system of Red Cross societies.

Did you know?

Henri Dunant donated to charity the money he was awarded for his Nobel Prize for Peace.

First Nobel Prize for Peace

Sadly, by 1867 Dunant had lost all his money and become ill, partly because of the efforts he had put into his humanitarian work. He remained in hospital for the last 18 years of his life. In 1901 he was awarded the first Nobel Prize for Peace.

Early work

World War I led to a considerable expansion of the ICRC's activities. In addition to its traditional work in helping wounded or sick soldiers, the ICRC extended its work to include prisoners of war (POWs).

Prisoners of war

The ICRC set up a special body, the International Prisoners-of-War Agency, to collect and pass on information about prisoners. ICRC delegates also visited many POW camps in order to check that prisoners were being held in reasonable and humane conditions.

These Red Cross workers are helping wounded soldiers during World War I.

Following the Geneva Conventions

During World War I, the ICRC also checked that the Geneva Conventions on wounded and shipwrecked soldiers and sailors were being followed. If not, the Red Cross privately notified the governments concerned. It did not make public comments because it had a rule of not taking sides in any fighting. It also worked to help civilians, particularly those living in enemy-occupied territory.

Did you know?

The use of poison gas between 1915 and 1918 was the first example of a weapon of mass destruction.

Protesting against inhumane treatment

Throughout the conflict, the ICRC was to protest against any inhumane treatment given to both the military and civilians. It also led a strong campaign against the use of chemical weapons such a gas attacks. Gas attacks were used for the first time during World War I, causing deaths and injuries on a scale that had never been seen before.

Core values of the Red Cross

Core values are the things that a person, group or organisation really believes in. The values are used to work out rules of behaviour. The Red Cross and Red Crescent Movement calls them Fundamental Principles. The Red Cross has seven Fundamental Principles and they are always written in exactly these words:

Humanity

The International Red Cross and Red Crescent Movement, born of a desire to bring assistance without **discrimination** to the wounded on the battlefield, endeavours, in its international and national capacity, to prevent and **alleviate** human suffering wherever it may be found. Its purpose is to protect life and health and ensure respect for the human being. It promotes mutual understanding, friendship, cooperation and lasting peace amongst all people.

Impartiality

It makes no discrimination as to nationality, race, religious beliefs, class or political opinions. It endeavours to relieve the suffering of individuals, being guided solely by their needs, and to give priority to the most urgent cases of distress.

The Fundamental Principles were proclaimed in Vienna in 1965.

The Red Cross aims to help all those in need, regardless of their ethnic background.

Glossary words

discrimination unfair treatment because of race, religion or other unjust reason

alleviate lessen

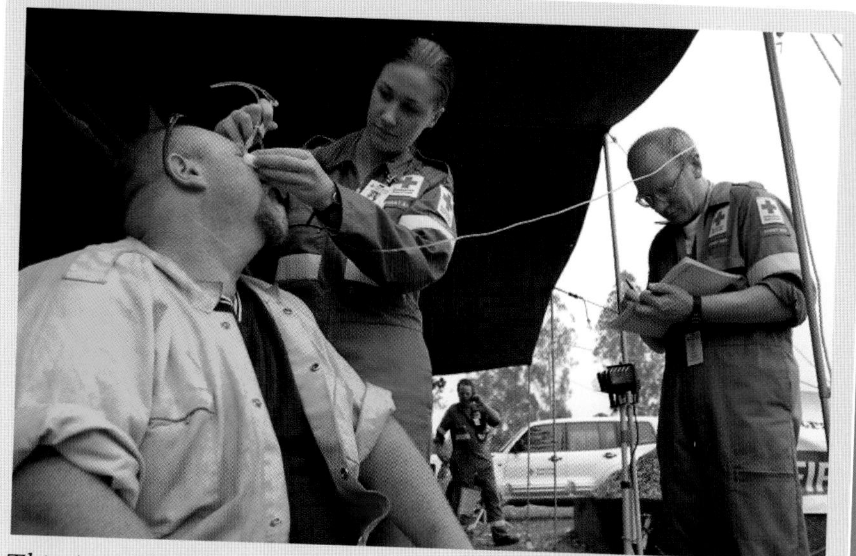

This Australian Red Cross unit is providing first aid to emergency services personnel.

Neutrality

In order to continue to enjoy the confidence of all, the movement may not take sides in hostilities or engage at any time in controversies of a political, racial, religious or **ideological** nature.

Independence

The movement is independent. The national societies, while **auxiliaries** in the humanitarian services of their governments and subject to the laws of their respective countries, must always maintain their autonomy so that they may be able at all times to act in accordance with the principles of the movement.

Voluntary service

It is a voluntary relief movement not prompted in any manner by desire for gain.

Unity

There can be only one Red Cross or Red Crescent Society in any one country. It must be open to all. It must carry on its humanitarian work throughout its territory.

Universality

The International Red Cross and Red Crescent Movement, in which all societies have equal status and share equal responsibilities and duties in helping each other, is worldwide.

Did you know?

In 2002, the ICRC collected 500 000 messages and was able to distribute 450 000 of them to restore contact between families separated by war.

Glossary words

ideological
based on one particular set of ideas

auxiliaries
assistant organisations

Where in the world is the Red Cross?

Today there is a Red Cross or Red Crescent Society active in nearly every country in the world. This map shows the countries and regions in which the International Committee of the Red Cross and the International Federation operate. A full listing of Red Cross and Red Crescent Societies can be found at www.ifrc.org.

Timeline

The Red Cross has been working to help people since it began in 1863.

1863	International Committee of the Red Cross is created in Switzerland.
1864	First Geneva Convention is established, governing how non-combatants should be treated in times of conflict.
1901–18	Henri Dunant and the International Committee of the Red Cross are both awarded the Nobel Prize for Peace.
1919	The League of Red Cross Societies, which is later renamed the International Federation of Red Cross and Red Crescent Societies, is founded after World War I.
1920–39	Work on social changes in Europe and the USA after World War I and the Great Depression.
1940–59	Beginnings of the blood donation program as a response to World War II and its after-effects.
1949	The ICRC develops a fourth Geneva Convention and revises the previous three.
1960–79	Adoption of the Fundamental Principles. Responses to the Vietnam War, the apartheid policy in South Africa and the nuclear disaster at Three Mile Island in the United States of America.
1977	Two additional Protocols (agreements) to the Geneva Conventions are adopted.
1980	Red Cross enters its second century of service. Increased use of technology, such as computers, and community education programs, such as HIV/AIDS education.
1991–99	Major operations in the Balkans, Rwanda and Kosovo.
1997–2004	150 governments sign a treaty banning landmines.
2002	The ICRC begins visiting prisoners accused of terrorism held in Bagram (Afghanistan), and Guantanamo Bay (Cuba).
2003–04	The ICRC employs thousands of local and foreign staff to fight the effects of famine, disease and war in 29 African countries.

to countries and regions

CIFIC REGION
stralia, Cook Islands, Kiribati, Marshall ands, Micronesia, uru, New Zealand, au, Papua New Guinea, noa, Solomon Islands, ga, Tuvalu, Vanuatu

IA AND THE DDLE EAST
hanistan, Armenia, rbaijan, Bahrain, ngladesh, Bhutan, nei, Burma (Myanmar), nbodia, China, t Timor, India, onesia, Israel and Occupied and onomous Territories, an, Kazakhstan, wait, Kyrgyzstan, Laos, laysia, Maldives, ngolia, Nepal, th Korea, Oman, kistan, Philippines, ar, Saudi Arabia, gapore, South Korea, Lanka, Syria, kistan, Thailand, kmenistan, United b Emirates, bekistan, Vietnam, nen

ROPE
ania, Belarus, Belgium, snia–Herzegovina, garia, Croatia, Czech oublic, Estonia, France, orgia, Hungary, Latvia, uania, Macedonia, ldova, Poland, nania, Serbia and ntenegro, Slovakia, venia, Turkey

AFRICA
Algeria , Angola, Benin, Botswana, Burkina Faso, Burundi, Cameroon, Cape Verde, Central African Republic, Chad, Comoros, Democratic Republic of the Congo, Côte d'Ivoire, Djibouti, Egypt, Equatorial Guinea, Eritrea, Ethiopia, Gabon, Gambia, Ghana, Guinea, Guinea-Bissau, Kenya, Lesotho, Liberia, Libya, Madagascar, Malawi, Mali, Mauritania, Mauritius, Morocco, Mozambique, Namibia, Niger, Nigeria, Rwanda, Sao Tome and Principe, Senegal, Seychelles, Sierra Leone, Somalia, South Africa, Sudan, Swaziland, Tanzania, Togo, Tunisia, Uganda, Zambia, Zimbabwe

NORTH AND CENTRAL AMERICA
Belize, Costa Rica, Cuba, Dominican Republic, El Salvador, Grenada, Guatemala, Haiti, Honduras, Jamaica, Mexico, Panama, United States of America

SOUTH AMERICA
Argentina, Bolivia, Brazil, Chile, Colombia, Ecuador, Guyana, Nicaragua, Paraguay, Peru, Suriname, Uruguay, Venezuela

Concerns, campaigns and classic actions

The Red Cross is concerned about a range of humanitarian problems throughout the world. It identifies specific campaigns and takes action accordingly.

CONCERNS

Problems caused by conflicts

The Red Cross and Red Crescent are concerned about the many problems that are caused by wars and conflicts. The sick and wounded need care and treatment. People will need food, clothing and shelter. Families may have been separated and members will have lost contact with each other. Prisoners of war may not be properly treated.

In 2004, Red Crescent volunteers provided tents, plastic sheeting, blankets and household items in this camp for displaced people in the conflict-torn region of Darfur, in Sudan.

CAMPAIGNS

The International Red Cross began with the results of a war, and it has been active in this area ever since. The International Committee of the Red Cross has special status in international law to protect and assist victims of conflicts. The Committee sends representatives into war zones to perform five main tasks:

1. The ICRC sends medical staff, supplies and equipment when local services cannot cope with the wounded. Under the sign of the Red Cross or Red Crescent, staff and patients are entitled to special protection and access to conflict zones. No building or vehicle carrying these signs should ever be attacked.
2. The ICRC works with the local Red Cross society to provide water, clothes, food and shelter to civilians who have been forced out of their homes by the fighting. Sometimes this type of help is needeed for a long time after the fighting stops.

CAMPAIGNS

3. The ICRC visits prisoners of war and speaks to them in private. They also check on their health and living conditions. At all times, Red Cross visitors remain strictly neutral, but they do negotiate privately with the authorities of the country for improvements if necessary. The ICRC also registers prisoners' names so that their families can be informed of their situation.
4. The ICRC runs a tracing service to help families that have been separated. This can include identifying bodies so that at least people know what has happened to someone they loved. They can exchange messages between relatives in different parts of a country or in other countries where they may have been forced to take shelter. The Red Cross can also arrange reunions, sometimes by bringing people home to their own countries.
5. Both the ICRC and national groups monitor and educate military and civilian groups about the rules of war set down in the Geneva Conventions. This is done in peacetime as well as in times of war.

Classic action

After the bombings in Bali, Indonesia, in 2002, there was much disruption and chaos. People did not know if their relatives had been at the scene of the explosions. Seven weeks after the bombings, 19 Indonesians were still missing. The Indonesian Red Cross helped to find out what had happened to them.

The Red Cross helped families to find out what happened to their loved ones as a result of the bombings in Bali in 2002.

CONCERNS

Community members in need of help

Even in peacetime, the Red Cross is concerned about the many people in the community who need help. These include children, the elderly and the sick.

CAMPAIGNS

National Red Cross and Red Crescent societies provide a range of services in their local communities.

Blood service

One of the best known of these is the blood service. In countries around the world, donors are screened and blood stocks are collected and cared for. The Red Cross not only provides blood for **transfusions**, but also **plasma** and tissue for transplants.

Dealing with major disasters

It is vital that communities are informed about how to prepare for and respond to major disasters. National Red Cross societies work with community groups and individuals to educate and to attempt to limit damage when disasters do occur.

Pet therapy

In hospitals and nursing homes, Red Cross members visit sick people and help with small tasks such as mail or shopping. Programs using pets as therapy have also been a great success.

Shelter for the homeless

In some countries the Red Cross provides shelter for homeless people. They offer them a meal, washing facilities and a bed for the night.

Transport services

In many countries the Red Cross provides a transport service for people who cannot drive. People are taken to medical and hospital appointments or to do essential shopping.

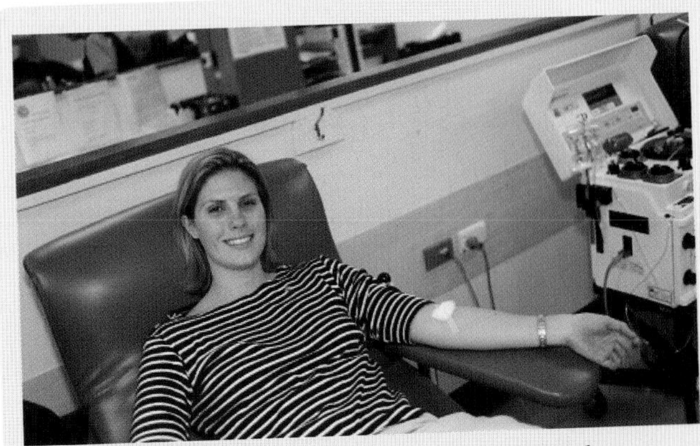

The Red Cross is well known for its blood collection service.

Glossary words

transfusions
transferring of blood from one person to another

plasma
a clear fluid in the blood that carries blood cells

CAMPAIGNS

Youth and education services

Youth and education services are an important part of Red Cross community work. Young people learn about the work of the Red Cross and Red Crescent Movement, international friendship, service to the community, as well as health and safety. Junior Red Cross classes are held in primary and secondary schools with a range of educational materials.

First-aid training

Both young people and adults often gain first-aid qualifications by attending Red Cross classes. This has saved many lives.

Support services

The Red Cross provides a range of support services for other vulnerable members of the community. In various ways, the Red Cross can help people caring for disabled relatives, mothers with young babies, the mentally ill and refugees.

Tracing service

National Red Cross and Red Crescent Societies assist the Federation and the ICRC in tracing people missing as a result of conflict or disaster.

Helping people to understand their rights

It is very important that people understand their rights in times of conflict and disaster. As the guardian of the Geneva Conventions, the Red Cross provides information to military groups and to all civilians about **International Humanitarian Law** and the role of Red Cross in times of crisis and peace.

Classic action

Maggie, a golden retriever, is a therapy dog. She wears a special identity tag and visits nursing homes to give special attention to elderly and disabled people. These patients respond so well to the visits that it has beneficial effects on their health.

These therapy dogs are being trained to work with the American Red Cross Animal Assisted Crisis Response Team.

Glossary words

International Humanitarian Law
the laws of war

CONCERNS

Responding to disasters

The Red Cross is concerned about the effects of natural disasters. Floods, droughts, earthquakes and volcanic eruptions cause destruction and death all over the world. Medical care and basic necessities of life are needed urgently in these situations.

CAMPAIGNS

The International Federation of Red Cross and Red Crescent Societies is alarmed at the increasing frequency of disasters experienced around the world. Because of this, they are giving increasing attention to disaster management work. This includes disaster preparedness and disaster response.

Disaster preparedness programs aim to educate communities who live in disaster-prone areas. They explain to community members the risks they may face, how they can try to protect themselves and what they can do if a disaster strikes. For example, communications systems can be put in place to send early warning of an approaching disaster, such as a cyclone, so that people have more time to prepare. Training programs can be run for local volunteers, who can then act as leaders in dangerous situations. Community education can be also made available to teach adults and children how to avoid death or injury during and after a disaster.

National groups also monitor their own performance in previous disasters. They examine what they were able to do and look at how they might improve their responses if another similar disaster occurs.

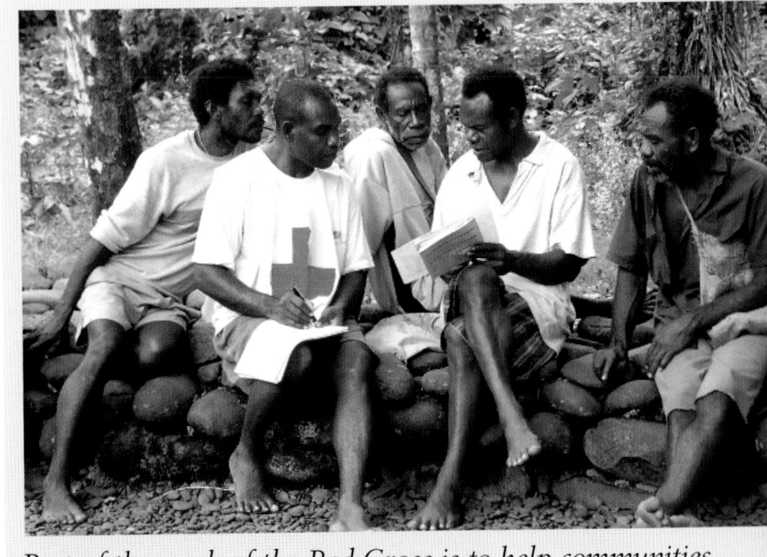

Part of the work of the Red Cross is to help communities learn how to prepare for disaster situations. This is part of the Weather Coast Assessment Relief Team.

CAMPAIGNS

Disasters can affect a single household or a whole country. Each Red Cross or Red Crescent society has local volunteers trained to respond. A local response is always the first step. If it is a major disaster, the national society can ask for help and support from the International Federation if required. They use this procedure:

1. An international fundraising appeal is launched.
2. Societies around the world are asked to help.
3. Specialists in medicine, **logistics** and water are sought, and other relief workers are sent out.
4. Equipment such as food, clothing, blankets, tents and medicine are either bought locally or shipped in, depending on the circumstances.

When the first crisis has begun to ease, extra help may be sent in. The International Red Cross sets in place programs to assess the response and to find ways to improve their work in the future. Local societies also have some involvement in this process.

Classic action

In January 2001, a violent earthquake struck Gujarat, in India. It was the worst such disaster for 50 years. It killed 20 000 people and injured another 166 000. The Indian Red Cross immediately responded, but the disaster was so great that international help was needed. Tonnes of relief supplies were delivered and whole towns were eventually rebuilt.

The earthquake in Gujarat, India, left devastating effects.

Glossary word

logistics
organisation of people, equipment and procedures to get a job done

International Humanitarian Law

In times of war, it is vital that governments, military forces and citizens understand and respect laws about human rights. In many cases, this does not happen.

CAMPAIGNS

The International Committee of the Red Cross is the guardian of the Geneva Conventions. No other organisation has this role. The first Geneva Convention was signed by 12 governments in Switzerland over 100 years ago. Today there are four Geneva Conventions. They set out rules to protect these groups:

- wounded and sick soldiers on land (1864)
- wounded and shipwrecked sailors (1906)
- prisoners of war (1929)
- civilians (1949).

In 1977, two additions, called Protocols, gave further protection to victims of war. They have been signed by 190 countries, and are the basis of International Humanitarian Law.

The ICRC has the basic responsibility of making sure that governments understand what the Geneva Conventions require them to do. They also need to educate members of the general public who might influence others. These include teachers, media people and politicians. It is important that all groups understand that the Red Cross is strictly neutral, and that its symbols are respected as signs of protection.

The Red Cross emblem is recognised as a symbol of protection on the battlefield.

These are the agreements that form the Geneva Conventions:

- Sick or wounded soldiers must be protected and given treatment. Medical and religious personnel should never be attacked. Buildings and vehicles showing the Red Cross or Red Crescent emblems must be protected.
- The same rules as listed in the first Convention (above) also apply to those at sea.
- Prisoners of war must be treated humanely. They should not be threatened or tortured. They should be registered and allowed to contact their families. After the war they should be released.
- Civilians should not be deliberately attacked or made part of the fighting. Their property should not be destroyed or stolen. They should not be used as hostages or hurt for revenge.

Classic action

At Guantanamo Bay, Cuba, there is a prison that currently holds around 600 people who were captured during the war in Afghanistan. The American government does not call them prisoners of war, but has said they will be treated according to the Geneva Conventions. The prisoners are visited regularly by teams from the ICRC. The Committee checks the conditions inside the prison, and reports its findings and suggestions on improvements to the detaining authorities. They also deliver messages for the detainees.

This prisoner is being transported by military police after being interrogated at the Guantanamo Bay prison in Cuba.

The people of the Red Cross

The Red Cross helps people and communities all over the world. Here are four volunteers who use their own specialised skills to help in different situations.

DON ATKINSON Water and sanitation engineer

These Red Cross workers are distributing supplies to help people affected by the floods in Mozambique.

Don Atkinson works as an environmental health officer with a local council in Australia, but spends his holidays and any other leave he can get working for the Red Cross. After reading in a local newsletter about the need for experts to work overseas, Don applied and left on his first mission to Zimbabwe in Africa in 2000.

While working on water and **sanitation** projects in Zimbabwe and Kenya, Don was also asked to help in nearby Mozambique, which was being devastated by floods at the time. He was in fact caught by the floods himself and had to make a fast drive out of the area in a four-wheel-drive vehicle. He quickly returned to help rebuild water and sanitation systems to prevent disease.

Don's most recent mission was to Jordan, on the border of Iraq, where thousands of people were expected to be escaping from the war in 2003. Don worked with other humanitarian organisations, amongst riots and bomb threats, to help set up water systems for refugee camps that were being prepared. It turned out that there were not as many refugees as expected and Don was able to return home.

Did you know?

Floods in Mozambique left 45 000 people homeless.

Glossary word

sanitation
drainage and disposal of sewage

Don has now completed four missions for the Red Cross. While waiting for his next assignment, he takes training courses to improve his skills and be better prepared for future disasters. Don's family has come to accept that Red Cross work is essential for his well being, and realises that it is now a part of their lives. Whenever Don is away, they all pull together to support him and each other. Don thrives on the challenges that his work provides and on the excitement of achieving something constructive. He also enjoys being involved in other cultures and being able to use his abilities to help them.

There are sometimes risks involved, particularly when working near war zones. Red Cross workers have sometimes been attacked. Don hopes that more education programs in the future will improve this situation, and that people will better understand the wonderful work that the organisation does.

Did you know?

Cholera is a disease spread by poor water supplies and a lack of proper toilets. When it breaks out, it can kill more than 55 per cent of a community.

Don Atkinson helps to build systems that provide clean drinking water.

DOCTOR MERRITT SCHREIBER Psychologist

Merritt 'Chip' Schreiber currently works as a member of a special Critical Response Team of volunteers who respond to such things as plane crashes and actions by terrorists.

Dr Merritt 'Chip' Schreiber lives with his family in Southern California, where he works as a volunteer for the American Red Cross Mental Health Team. He joined the organisation in 1993 when he began designing a counselling service for children affected by a major disaster at that time. Many children had lost their homes or been affected in some other way by a huge fire which had burned out more than 8000 hectares (20 000 acres). This experience was so rewarding that Chip began changing his career to work with victims of disasters or those who were dealing with the loss of loved ones from such disasters.

All of Chip's skills and training were needed after the terrorist attacks on 11 September 2001. He went straight to the airport at Los Angeles, where three of the crashed planes had been due to land. He met relatives of victims, set up counselling and arranged for translators as needed. He was also there just to listen, so people could talk about the loved ones who had been killed. Chip felt very privileged that he had been given the chance to do something to help at this time.

Did you know?

By March 2002, the Red Cross had spent over $500 million in dealing with the attacks on 11 September 2001.The Red Cross provided:

- health and mental health services for 361 000 people
- money for families who had lost members, houses or jobs
- 14 million meals.

A victim of the terrorist attacks in the United States in 2001 is being carried by these fire fighters. A Red Cross chaplain (top right) is following them.

The American Red Cross has a saying: 'Help can't wait'. Chip is proud to be a part of that process, even though disaster counselling is very difficult and emotional work. He was especially touched when one of the families he had helped sent a donation to the Red Cross to thank them. Chip's own children, even though they don't like him to be away from them, are starting to raise money for the Red Cross and to help others in their own ways.

Chip has lots of plans for future Red Cross work. He gives talks to children in schools, and to police, fire and emergency medical people about working together and sharing information during big emergencies. He also encourages other psychologists and mental health workers to volunteer with the Red Cross and get involved in their local town's emergency plans. He now has a new job at the University of California in Los Angeles, where he is developing better ways to help children and families cope with disasters.

Did you know?

Each year, the American Red Cross responds immediately to more than 67 000 disasters including fires, hurricanes, floods, earthquakes, tornadoes, hazardous-materials spills, transportation accidents, explosions and other natural and man-made disasters.

BELINDA BARNARD Youth worker

As well as working for the Red Cross, Belinda Barnard also works at a women's legal centre and as an advocate for people with disabilities.

Belinda Barnard first began working for the Red Cross in primary school when she collected donations as a volunteer, before later becoming involved in the areas of youth and International Humanitarian Law. After completing an arts/law degree at university, she travelled to Cambodia, where she worked for a year as a delegate with the International Federation of Red Cross and Red Crescent Societies. During this time, she received a small wage funded by the Australian government.

In Cambodia, Belinda worked with the Red Cross Youth program. This program is based mostly in secondary schools, across many parts of the country, and covers a variety of subjects. Belinda helped develop courses that included landmine awareness, HIV/AIDS prevention, first aid and health care. She spent a lot of time travelling to small remote villages throughout Cambodia, and learnt a lot about the language and culture of the people. She also met and worked with other Red Cross delegates from Finland, Japan, the United States of America and Sweden, which gave her even more experience at international communication and teamwork.

Did you know?

Every month, around 60 people are injured by landmines in Cambodia.

When Belinda first arrived in Cambodia, the country was suffering from the effects of the worst floods in 75 years. She immediately began helping with the disaster response and emergency relief, and for a while was afraid that she would not be able to do all that was needed.

It was a new experience for Belinda to be away from her family, and she missed not being able to share all the family events that were happening back home. But getting through that difficult time and finding that she was able to provide valuable help to Cambodians in need was a very satisfying experience.

Belinda finds her Red Cross work incredibly rewarding. While it can be exhausting, she believes it is important to meet the needs of people in difficult situations. Belinda would like to see more young people involved in Red Cross work, and she would like to go overseas again as a Red Cross delegate when her work in Australia permits.

Did you know?

In 2002–03, the Australian Red Cross Society had 37 886 members, including 4287 Junior Red Cross members.

The Red Cross provides a youth education service in Cambodia.

JANE CLARKE Tracing service

Jane Clarke regards her work at the Red Cross as much more than just a job.

Jane Clarke works in the tracing section of the International Committee of the Red Cross in Sarajevo, Bosnia. Her job is to help people who have been separated from their families to find them again, or to at least find out what has happened to them.

Jane says her work can be very rewarding, but can also be very sad. One of Jane's happiest jobs was to help reunite two small boys from Zaire, in Africa, with their uncle in Australia. The boys were only nine and seven years of age when both their parents were killed in a **civil war**. They walked for weeks to find some safety in a neighbouring country, until Red Cross workers eventually found them living under a truck. The boys now live with their uncle in Australia.

In Bosnia, many stories do not end happily. During the war there in 1996, thousands of people were killed and thousands more disappeared without trace. Many of the missing are male, and many of these were also the main income-earners of their families. Mothers and children had to relocate, often several times, without knowing what had happened to their husbands, fathers and brothers.

Unfortunately, often the only way people can find out about missing family members is by identifying clothes or belongings that have been found in mass graves. The Bosnian Red Cross arranges for these clothes to be carefully sorted and washed, and then photographed. Families can look through the books to see if they can identify any items, and try to at least put an end to their uncertainty.

Did you know?

When the war in Bosnia ended, 20 000 people were missing. Only 4000 of these people have been traced.

Glossary word

civil war
war between different groups within a country

The Red Cross supplies food to people, such as these children in Kosovo, who might otherwise have none.

Jane has had to learn to keep her feelings under control so that she can continue to help other families. Bosnia is slowly being rebuilt, although many young people still leave to get jobs or better education in other countries. Bullet holes are everywhere and security forces still maintain order. There is danger from unexploded bombs and landmines.

Although Jane misses her family in Australia, she would never consider giving up her work with the Red Cross. She follows the principles of the organisation, even though it can sometimes be hard to stay strictly neutral and not to take sides. She finds it a challenge, but one she is happy to undertake.

Did you know?

Since the mid 1990s, the American Red Cross has managed a large-scale supplemental feeding program for the elderly in both the Federation of Bosnia–Herzegovina and the Serbska Republika. They have distributed more than 20 000 metric tons of food valued at more than $17 million.

What can you do?

Junior Red Cross and Red Crescent groups have existed since the late 1800s. They are often attached to schools.

Wartime

Junior Red Cross and Red Crescent groups have been particularly well supported in times of war. During these times children helped to make and pack clothes and food to be sent to affected areas. They also visited hospitals in their own areas.

Peacetime

In peacetime, Junior Red Cross and Red Crescent groups continue to do important work. They are active around the world. In a Junior Red Cross group, members might:

- learn about other countries and international issues
- learn first aid or water safety
- take part in a program to help someone in their community
- learn the skills of leadership and take part in making decisions about the future
- donate blood if they are old enough, or help to organise blood donations
- learn what to do in the case of a large or small disaster.

An Australian Junior Red Cross group prepares 'Trauma Teddies' to parade at a local show.

Information for young people

National Red Cross societies have officers who work specifically on activities for young people and who support young volunteers in many different roles. They produce magazines, project material and information to be used in Junior Red Cross classes. In many countries there are also web sites with information and activities for people aged from 8 to 25 years. These include:

www.ifrc.org
www.icrc.org
www.redcross.org
www.redcross.org.au

Glossary

alleviate	lessen
apartheid	a policy of separation of people based on race
auxiliaries	assistant organisations
civil war	war between different groups within a country
community development	the building of stronger communities (e.g. through help for women's groups or support for teenagers)
discrimination	unfair treatment because of race, religion or other unjust reason
Geneva Conventions	ways of behaving in wars (e.g. towards prisoners) accepted and agreed to by the countries that have signed the documents
HIV/AIDS	a virus that stops the body from fighting against infections
human rights	a set of rights, such as the right to a fair trial, laid down by the United Nations
humanely	considerately, compassionately
humanitarian	devoted to people's welfare and the promotion of social reform
ideological	based on one particular set of ideas
International Humanitarian Law	the laws of war
logistics	organisation of people, equipment and procedures to get a job done
neutral	not taking either side in an argument or fight
Nobel Prize for Peace	an award presented by the Nobel Committee in Sweden to a person or group who gives the greatest benefit to humankind
plasma	a clear fluid in the blood that carries blood cells
sanitation	drainage and disposal of sewage
transfusions	transferring of blood from one person to another
volunteers	people who donate their time to a cause

Index